National Park Memory Book

Unqualified Hikers

KEEP CLOSE TO NATURE'S HEART... AND BREAK CLEAR AWAY, ONCE IN A WHILE, AND CLIMB A MOUNTAIN OR

SPEND A WEEK IN THE WOODS. WASH YOUR SPIRIT CLEAN...

- JOHN MUIR

ACADIA NATIONAL PARK

(Park Sign or Photo Here)

Trails We Hiked:

_____ Distance: _____ Elev:_____

_____ Distance: _____ Elev:_____

_____ Distance: _____ Elev:_____

_____ Distance: _____ Elev:_____

Places We Saw:

_____

_____

_____

Places We Stayed:

_____

_____

_____

_____ - _____

_____ - _____

Our Favorite Memory:

_____
_____
_____
_____
_____
_____

Things we learned:

_____
_____
_____
_____
_____
_____
_____
_____
_____
_____
_____

Notes For Next Time:

_____
_____
_____
_____
_____
_____
_____
_____
_____

ARCHES NATIONAL PARK

(Park Sign or Photo Here)

Trails We Hiked:

_____ Distance: _____ Elev:_____

_____ Distance: _____ Elev:_____

_____ Distance: _____ Elev:_____

_____ Distance: _____ Elev:_____

Places We Saw:

_____

_____

_____

Places We Stayed:

_____

_____

_____

_____ - _____

_____ - _____

Our Favorite Memory:

_____
_____
_____
_____
_____
_____

Things we learned:

_____
_____
_____
_____
_____
_____
_____
_____
_____
_____
_____

Notes For Next Time:

_____
_____
_____
_____
_____
_____
_____
_____
_____

BADLANDS NATIONAL PARK

(Park Sign or Photo Here)

Trails We Hiked:

_____ Distance: _____ Elev:_____

_____ Distance: _____ Elev:_____

_____ Distance: _____ Elev:_____

_____ Distance: _____ Elev:_____

Places We Saw: **Places We Stayed:**

_____   _____

_____   _____

_____   _____

Dates We Visited:

_____ - _____

_____ - _____

Our Favorite Memory:

_____
_____
_____
_____
_____
_____

Things we learned:

_____
_____
_____
_____
_____
_____
_____
_____
_____
_____
_____
_____

Notes For Next Time:

_____
_____
_____
_____
_____
_____
_____
_____
_____
_____

BIG BEND NATIONAL PARK

(Park Sign or Photo Here)

Trails We Hiked:

_____ Distance: _____ Elev:_____

_____ Distance: _____ Elev:_____

_____ Distance: _____ Elev:_____

_____ Distance: _____ Elev:_____

Places We Saw:

_____

_____

_____

Places We Stayed:

_____

_____

_____

Dates We Visited:

_____ - _____

_____ - _____

Our Favorite Memory:

_____

_____

_____

_____

_____

Things we learned:

_____

_____

_____

_____

_____

_____

_____

_____

_____

_____

Notes For Next Time:

_____

_____

_____

_____

_____

_____

_____

_____

_____

BISCAYNE NATIONAL PARK

(Park Sign or Photo Here)

Trails We Hiked:

_____ Distance: _____ Elev:_____

_____ Distance: _____ Elev:_____

_____ Distance: _____ Elev:_____

_____ Distance: _____ Elev:_____

Places We Saw:

_____

_____

_____

Places We Stayed:

_____

_____

_____

Dates We Visited:

_____ - _____

_____ - _____

Our Favorite Memory:

_____
_____
_____
_____
_____
_____

Things we learned:

_____
_____
_____
_____
_____
_____
_____
_____
_____
_____
_____

Notes For Next Time:

_____
_____
_____
_____
_____
_____
_____
_____
_____

BLACK CANYON OF THE GUNNISON NATIONAL PARK

(Park Sign or Photo Here)

Trails We Hiked:

_____ Distance: _____ Elev:_____

_____ Distance: _____ Elev:_____

_____ Distance: _____ Elev:_____

_____ Distance: _____ Elev:_____

Places We Saw:

_____

_____

_____

Places We Stayed:

_____

_____

_____

Dates We Visited:

_____ - _____

_____ - _____

Our Favorite Memory:

_____
_____
_____
_____
_____
_____

Things we learned:

_____
_____
_____
_____
_____
_____
_____
_____
_____
_____
_____

Notes For Next Time:

_____
_____
_____
_____
_____
_____
_____
_____
_____

BRYCE CANYON NATIONAL PARK

(Park Sign or Photo Here)

Trails We Hiked:

_____ Distance: _____ Elev:_____

_____ Distance: _____ Elev:_____

_____ Distance: _____ Elev:_____

_____ Distance: _____ Elev:_____

Places We Saw:

_____

_____

_____

Places We Stayed:

_____

_____

_____

Dates We Visited:

_____ - _____

_____ - _____

Our Favorite Memory:

_____
_____
_____
_____
_____
_____

Things we learned:

_____
_____
_____
_____
_____
_____
_____
_____
_____
_____
_____
_____

Notes For Next Time:

_____
_____
_____
_____
_____
_____
_____
_____
_____
_____

CANYONLANDS NATIONAL PARK

(Park Sign or Photo Here)

Trails We Hiked:

_____ Distance: _____ Elev:_____

_____ Distance: _____ Elev:_____

_____ Distance: _____ Elev:_____

_____ Distance: _____ Elev:_____

Places We Saw:

_____

_____

_____

Places We Stayed:

_____

_____

_____

Dates We Visited:

_____ - _____

_____ - _____

Our Favorite Memory:

_____
_____
_____
_____
_____
_____

Things we learned:

_____
_____
_____
_____
_____
_____
_____
_____
_____
_____
_____
_____

Notes For Next Time:

_____
_____
_____
_____
_____
_____
_____
_____
_____

CAPITOL REEF NATIONAL PARK

(Park Sign or Photo Here)

Trails We Hiked:

_____ Distance: _____ Elev:_____

_____ Distance: _____ Elev:_____

_____ Distance: _____ Elev:_____

_____ Distance: _____ Elev:_____

Places We Saw:

_____

_____

_____

Places We Stayed:

_____

_____

_____

Dates We Visited:

_____ - _____

_____ - _____

Our Favorite Memory:

_____

_____

_____

_____

_____

Things we learned:

_____

_____

_____

_____

_____

_____

_____

_____

_____

_____

Notes For Next Time:

_____

_____

_____

_____

_____

_____

_____

_____

CARLSBAD CAVERNS NATIONAL PARK

(Park Sign or Photo Here)

Trails We Hiked:

_____ Distance: _____ Elev:_____

_____ Distance: _____ Elev:_____

_____ Distance: _____ Elev:_____

_____ Distance: _____ Elev:_____

Places We Saw:

_____

_____

_____

Places We Stayed:

_____

_____

_____

Dates We Visited:

_____ - _____

_____ - _____

Our Favorite Memory:

_____
_____
_____
_____
_____

Things we learned:

_____
_____
_____
_____
_____
_____
_____
_____
_____
_____

Notes For Next Time:

_____
_____
_____
_____
_____
_____
_____
_____

CHANNEL ISLANDS NATIONAL PARK

(Park Sign or Photo Here)

Trails We Hiked:

_____ Distance: _____ Elev:_____

_____ Distance: _____ Elev:_____

_____ Distance: _____ Elev:_____

_____ Distance: _____ Elev:_____

Places We Saw:

_____

_____

_____

Places We Stayed:

_____

_____

_____

Dates We Visited:

_____ - _____

_____ - _____

Our Favorite Memory:

_____
_____
_____
_____
_____
_____

Things we learned:

_____
_____
_____
_____
_____
_____
_____
_____
_____
_____
_____

Notes For Next Time:

_____
_____
_____
_____
_____
_____
_____
_____
_____

CONGAREE NATIONAL PARK

(Park Sign or Photo Here)

Trails We Hiked:

_____ Distance: _____ Elev:_____

_____ Distance: _____ Elev:_____

_____ Distance: _____ Elev:_____

_____ Distance: _____ Elev:_____

Places We Saw:

_____

_____

_____

Places We Stayed:

_____

_____

_____

_____ - _____

_____ - _____

Our Favorite Memory:

_____
_____
_____
_____
_____
_____

Things we learned:

_____
_____
_____
_____
_____
_____
_____
_____
_____
_____
_____

Notes For Next Time:

_____
_____
_____
_____
_____
_____
_____
_____
_____

CRATER LAKE NATIONAL PARK

(Park Sign or Photo Here)

Trails We Hiked:

_____ Distance: _____ Elev:_____

_____ Distance: _____ Elev:_____

_____ Distance: _____ Elev:_____

_____ Distance: _____ Elev:_____

Places We Saw: **Places We Stayed:**

_____   _____

_____   _____

_____   _____

Dates We Visited:

_____ - _____

_____ - _____

Our Favorite Memory:

_____
_____
_____
_____
_____
_____

Things we learned:

_____
_____
_____
_____
_____
_____
_____
_____
_____
_____
_____

Notes For Next Time:

_____
_____
_____
_____
_____
_____
_____
_____
_____

CUYAHOGA VALLEY NATIONAL PARK

(Park Sign or Photo Here)

Trails We Hiked:

_____ Distance: _____ Elev:_____

_____ Distance: _____ Elev:_____

_____ Distance: _____ Elev:_____

_____ Distance: _____ Elev:_____

Places We Saw:

_____

_____

_____

Places We Stayed:

_____

_____

_____

Dates We Visited:

_____ - _____
_____ - _____

Our Favorite Memory:

_____
_____
_____
_____
_____

Things we learned:

_____
_____
_____
_____
_____
_____
_____
_____
_____
_____

Notes For Next Time:

_____
_____
_____
_____
_____
_____
_____
_____

DEATH VALLEY NATIONAL PARK

(Park Sign or Photo Here)

Trails We Hiked:

_____ Distance: _____ Elev:_____

_____ Distance: _____ Elev:_____

_____ Distance: _____ Elev:_____

_____ Distance: _____ Elev:_____

Places We Saw: **Places We Stayed:**

_____   _____

_____   _____

_____   _____

Dates We Visited:

_____ - _____

_____ - _____

Our Favorite Memory:

_____
_____
_____
_____
_____
_____

Things we learned:

_____
_____
_____
_____
_____
_____
_____
_____
_____
_____
_____

Notes For Next Time:

_____
_____
_____
_____
_____
_____
_____
_____
_____
_____

DENALI NATIONAL PARK

(Park Sign or Photo Here)

Trails We Hiked:

_____ Distance: _____ Elev:_____

_____ Distance: _____ Elev:_____

_____ Distance: _____ Elev:_____

_____ Distance: _____ Elev:_____

Places We Saw:

_____

_____

_____

Places We Stayed:

_____

_____

_____

Dates We Visited:

_____ - _____

_____ - _____

Our Favorite Memory:

_____
_____
_____
_____
_____

Things we learned:

_____
_____
_____
_____
_____
_____
_____
_____
_____
_____
_____

Notes For Next Time:

_____
_____
_____
_____
_____
_____
_____
_____
_____

DRY TORTUGAS NATIONAL PARK

(Park Sign or Photo Here)

Trails We Hiked:

_____ Distance: _____ Elev:_____

_____ Distance: _____ Elev:_____

_____ Distance: _____ Elev:_____

_____ Distance: _____ Elev:_____

Places We Saw:

_____

_____

_____

Places We Stayed:

_____

_____

_____

Dates We Visited:

_____ - _____

_____ - _____

Our Favorite Memory:

_____
_____
_____
_____
_____

Things we learned:

_____
_____
_____
_____
_____
_____
_____
_____
_____
_____

Notes For Next Time:

_____
_____
_____
_____
_____
_____
_____
_____
_____

EVERGLADES NATIONAL PARK

(Park Sign or Photo Here)

Trails We Hiked:

_____ Distance: _____ Elev:_____

_____ Distance: _____ Elev:_____

_____ Distance: _____ Elev:_____

_____ Distance: _____ Elev:_____

Places We Saw:

_____

_____

_____

Places We Stayed:

_____

_____

_____

Dates We Visited:

_____ - _____
_____ - _____

Our Favorite Memory:

_____
_____
_____
_____
_____
_____

Things we learned:

_____
_____
_____
_____
_____
_____
_____
_____
_____
_____
_____

Notes For Next Time:

_____
_____
_____
_____
_____
_____
_____
_____
_____
_____

GATES OF THE ARCTIC NATIONAL PARK

(Park Sign or Photo Here)

Trails We Hiked:

_____ Distance: _____ Elev:_____

_____ Distance: _____ Elev:_____

_____ Distance: _____ Elev:_____

_____ Distance: _____ Elev:_____

Places We Saw:

_____

_____

_____

Places We Stayed:

_____

_____

_____

Dates We Visited:

_____ - _____

_____ - _____

Our Favorite Memory:

_____
_____
_____
_____
_____
_____

Things we learned:

_____
_____
_____
_____
_____
_____
_____
_____
_____
_____
_____

Notes For Next Time:

_____
_____
_____
_____
_____
_____
_____
_____
_____

GATEWAY ARCH NATIONAL PARK

(Park Sign or Photo Here)

Trails We Hiked:

_____ Distance: _____ Elev:_____

_____ Distance: _____ Elev:_____

_____ Distance: _____ Elev:_____

_____ Distance: _____ Elev:_____

Places We Saw:

_____

_____

_____

Places We Stayed:

_____

_____

_____

_____ - _____

_____ - _____

Our Favorite Memory:

_____
_____
_____
_____
_____
_____

Things we learned:

_____
_____
_____
_____
_____
_____
_____
_____
_____
_____
_____

Notes For Next Time:

_____
_____
_____
_____
_____
_____
_____
_____
_____

GLACIER BAY NATIONAL PARK

(Park Sign or Photo Here)

Trails We Hiked:

_____ Distance: _____ Elev:_____

_____ Distance: _____ Elev:_____

_____ Distance: _____ Elev:_____

_____ Distance: _____ Elev:_____

Places We Saw:

_____

_____

_____

Places We Stayed:

_____

_____

_____

Dates We Visited:

_____ - _____

_____ - _____

Our Favorite Memory:

_____
_____
_____
_____
_____
_____

Things we learned:

_____
_____
_____
_____
_____
_____
_____
_____
_____
_____
_____
_____

Notes For Next Time:

_____
_____
_____
_____
_____
_____
_____
_____
_____

GLACIER NATIONAL PARK

(Park Sign or Photo Here)

Trails We Hiked:

_____ Distance: _____ Elev: _____

_____ Distance: _____ Elev: _____

_____ Distance: _____ Elev: _____

_____ Distance: _____ Elev: _____

Places We Saw: **Places We Stayed:**

_____   _____

_____   _____

_____   _____

Dates We Visited:

_____ - _____

_____ - _____

Our Favorite Memory:

_____

_____

_____

_____

_____

_____

Things we learned:

_____

_____

_____

_____

_____

_____

_____

_____

_____

_____

_____

Notes For Next Time:

_____

_____

_____

_____

_____

_____

_____

_____

_____

GRAND CANYON NATIONAL PARK

(Park Sign or Photo Here)

Trails We Hiked:

_____ Distance: _____ Elev:_____

_____ Distance: _____ Elev:_____

_____ Distance: _____ Elev:_____

_____ Distance: _____ Elev:_____

Places We Saw:

_____

_____

_____

Places We Stayed:

_____

_____

_____

Dates We Visited:

_____ - _____

_____ - _____

Our Favorite Memory:

_____
_____
_____
_____
_____
_____

Things we learned:

_____
_____
_____
_____
_____
_____
_____
_____
_____
_____
_____

Notes For Next Time:

_____
_____
_____
_____
_____
_____
_____
_____
_____
_____

GRAND TETON NATIONAL PARK

(Park Sign or Photo Here)

Trails We Hiked:

_____ Distance: _____ Elev:_____

_____ Distance: _____ Elev:_____

_____ Distance: _____ Elev:_____

_____ Distance: _____ Elev:_____

Places We Saw:

_____

_____

_____

Places We Stayed:

_____

_____

_____

Dates We Visited:

_____ - _____

_____ - _____

Our Favorite Memory:

_____
_____
_____
_____
_____
_____

Things we learned:

_____
_____
_____
_____
_____
_____
_____
_____
_____
_____
_____

Notes For Next Time:

_____
_____
_____
_____
_____
_____
_____
_____
_____

GREAT BASIN NATIONAL PARK

(Park Sign or Photo Here)

Trails We Hiked:

_____ Distance: _____ Elev: _____

_____ Distance: _____ Elev: _____

_____ Distance: _____ Elev: _____

_____ Distance: _____ Elev: _____

Places We Saw:

_____

_____

_____

Places We Stayed:

_____

_____

_____

Dates We Visited:

_____ - _____

_____ - _____

Our Favorite Memory:

_____
_____
_____
_____
_____
_____

Things we learned:

_____
_____
_____
_____
_____
_____
_____
_____
_____
_____
_____

Notes For Next Time:

_____
_____
_____
_____
_____
_____
_____
_____
_____
_____

GREAT SAND DUNES NATIONAL PARK

(Park Sign or Photo Here)

Trails We Hiked:

_____ Distance: _____ Elev:_____

_____ Distance: _____ Elev:_____

_____ Distance: _____ Elev:_____

_____ Distance: _____ Elev:_____

Places We Saw:

_____

_____

_____

Places We Stayed:

_____

_____

_____

Dates We Visited:

_____ - _____
_____ - _____

Our Favorite Memory:

_____
_____
_____
_____
_____
_____

Things we learned:

_____
_____
_____
_____
_____
_____
_____
_____
_____
_____
_____
_____

Notes For Next Time:

_____
_____
_____
_____
_____
_____
_____
_____
_____
_____

GREAT SMOKY MOUNTAINS NATIONAL PARK

(Park Sign or Photo Here)

Trails We Hiked:

_____ Distance: _____ Elev: _____

_____ Distance: _____ Elev: _____

_____ Distance: _____ Elev: _____

_____ Distance: _____ Elev: _____

Places We Saw:

_____

_____

_____

Places We Stayed:

_____

_____

_____

Dates We Visited:

_____ - _____
_____ - _____

Our Favorite Memory:

_____
_____
_____
_____
_____
_____

Things we learned:

_____
_____
_____
_____
_____
_____
_____
_____
_____
_____
_____

Notes For Next Time:

_____
_____
_____
_____
_____
_____
_____
_____
_____

GUADALUPE MOUNTAINS NATIONAL PARK

(Park Sign or Photo Here)

Trails We Hiked:

_____ Distance: _____ Elev:_____

_____ Distance: _____ Elev:_____

_____ Distance: _____ Elev:_____

_____ Distance: _____ Elev:_____

Places We Saw:

_____

_____

_____

Places We Stayed:

_____

_____

_____

_____ - _____

_____ - _____

Our Favorite Memory:

_____

_____

_____

_____

_____

Things we learned:

_____

_____

_____

_____

_____

_____

_____

_____

_____

_____

Notes For Next Time:

_____

_____

_____

_____

_____

_____

_____

_____

_____

HALEAKALA NATIONAL PARK

(Park Sign or Photo Here)

Trails We Hiked:

_____ Distance: _____ Elev:_____

_____ Distance: _____ Elev:_____

_____ Distance: _____ Elev:_____

_____ Distance: _____ Elev:_____

Places We Saw:

_____

_____

_____

Places We Stayed:

_____

_____

_____

Dates We Visited:

_____ - _____

_____ - _____

Our Favorite Memory:

_____
_____
_____
_____
_____

Things we learned:

_____
_____
_____
_____
_____
_____
_____
_____
_____

Notes For Next Time:

_____
_____
_____
_____
_____
_____
_____
_____

HAWAI'I VOLCANOS NATIONAL PARK

(Park Sign or Photo Here)

Trails We Hiked:

_____ Distance: _____ Elev:_____

_____ Distance: _____ Elev:_____

_____ Distance: _____ Elev:_____

_____ Distance: _____ Elev:_____

Places We Saw:

_____

_____

_____

Places We Stayed:

_____

_____

_____

Dates We Visited:

_____ - _____

_____ - _____

Our Favorite Memory:

_____
_____
_____
_____
_____
_____

Things we learned:

_____
_____
_____
_____
_____
_____
_____
_____
_____
_____

Notes For Next Time:

_____
_____
_____
_____
_____
_____
_____
_____
_____

HOT SPRINGS NATIONAL PARK

(Park Sign or Photo Here)

Trails We Hiked:

_____ Distance: _____ Elev:_____

_____ Distance: _____ Elev:_____

_____ Distance: _____ Elev:_____

_____ Distance: _____ Elev:_____

Places We Saw:

_____

_____

_____

Places We Stayed:

_____

_____

_____

Dates We Visited:

_____ - _____
_____ - _____

Our Favorite Memory:

_____
_____
_____
_____
_____

Things we learned:

_____
_____
_____
_____
_____
_____
_____
_____
_____
_____

Notes For Next Time:

_____
_____
_____
_____
_____
_____
_____
_____
_____

INDIANA DUNES NATIONAL PARK

(Park Sign or Photo Here)

Trails We Hiked:

_____ Distance: _____ Elev:_____

_____ Distance: _____ Elev:_____

_____ Distance: _____ Elev:_____

_____ Distance: _____ Elev:_____

Places We Saw:

_____

_____

_____

Places We Stayed:

_____

_____

_____

Dates We Visited:

_____ - _____

_____ - _____

Our Favorite Memory:

_____
_____
_____
_____
_____
_____

Things we learned:

_____
_____
_____
_____
_____
_____
_____
_____
_____
_____
_____

Notes For Next Time:

_____
_____
_____
_____
_____
_____
_____
_____
_____

ISLE ROYALE NATIONAL PARK

(Park Sign or Photo Here)

Trails We Hiked:

_____ Distance: _____ Elev:_____

_____ Distance: _____ Elev:_____

_____ Distance: _____ Elev:_____

_____ Distance: _____ Elev:_____

Places We Saw:

_____

_____

_____

Places We Stayed:

_____

_____

_____

Dates We Visited:

_____ - _____
_____ - _____

Our Favorite Memory:

_____
_____
_____
_____
_____
_____

Things we learned:

_____
_____
_____
_____
_____
_____
_____
_____
_____
_____
_____
_____

Notes For Next Time:

_____
_____
_____
_____
_____
_____
_____
_____
_____

JOSHUA TREE NATIONAL PARK

(Park Sign or Photo Here)

Trails We Hiked:

_____ Distance: _____ Elev:_____

_____ Distance: _____ Elev:_____

_____ Distance: _____ Elev:_____

_____ Distance: _____ Elev:_____

Places We Saw:

_____

_____

_____

Places We Stayed:

_____

_____

_____

Dates We Visited:

_____ - _____

_____ - _____

Our Favorite Memory:

_____
_____
_____
_____
_____

Things we learned:

_____
_____
_____
_____
_____
_____
_____
_____
_____
_____

Notes For Next Time:

_____
_____
_____
_____
_____
_____
_____
_____
_____

KATMAI NATIONAL PARK

(Park Sign or Photo Here)

Trails We Hiked:

_____ Distance: _____ Elev:_____

_____ Distance: _____ Elev:_____

_____ Distance: _____ Elev:_____

_____ Distance: _____ Elev:_____

Places We Saw:

_____

_____

_____

Places We Stayed:

_____

_____

_____

Dates We Visited:

_____ - _____
_____ - _____

Our Favorite Memory:

_____
_____
_____
_____
_____

Things we learned:

_____
_____
_____
_____
_____
_____
_____
_____
_____
_____
_____

Notes For Next Time:

_____
_____
_____
_____
_____
_____
_____
_____
_____

KENAI FJORDS NATIONAL PARK

(Park Sign or Photo Here)

Trails We Hiked:

_____ Distance: _____ Elev:_____

_____ Distance: _____ Elev:_____

_____ Distance: _____ Elev:_____

_____ Distance: _____ Elev:_____

Places We Saw:

_____

_____

_____

Places We Stayed:

_____

_____

_____

Dates We Visited:

_____ - _____

_____ - _____

Our Favorite Memory:

_____

_____

_____

_____

_____

Things we learned:

_____

_____

_____

_____

_____

_____

_____

_____

_____

_____

_____

Notes For Next Time:

_____

_____

_____

_____

_____

_____

_____

_____

_____

KINGS CANYON NATIONAL PARK

(Park Sign or Photo Here)

Trails We Hiked:

_____ Distance: _____ Elev:_____

_____ Distance: _____ Elev:_____

_____ Distance: _____ Elev:_____

_____ Distance: _____ Elev:_____

Places We Saw:

_____

_____

_____

Places We Stayed:

_____

_____

_____

_____ - _____

_____ - _____

Our Favorite Memory:

_____
_____
_____
_____
_____

Things we learned:

_____
_____
_____
_____
_____
_____
_____
_____
_____
_____

Notes For Next Time:

_____
_____
_____
_____
_____
_____
_____
_____

KOBUK VALLEY NATIONAL PARK

(Park Sign or Photo Here)

Trails We Hiked:

_____ Distance: _____ Elev:_____

_____ Distance: _____ Elev:_____

_____ Distance: _____ Elev:_____

_____ Distance: _____ Elev:_____

Places We Saw:

_____

_____

_____

Places We Stayed:

_____

_____

_____

Dates We Visited:

_____ - _____

_____ - _____

Our Favorite Memory:

_____

_____

_____

_____

_____

_____

Things we learned:

_____

_____

_____

_____

_____

_____

_____

_____

_____

_____

_____

_____

Notes For Next Time:

_____

_____

_____

_____

_____

_____

_____

_____

_____

LAKE CLARK NATIONAL PARK

(Park Sign or Photo Here)

Trails We Hiked:

_____ Distance: _____ Elev:_____

_____ Distance: _____ Elev:_____

_____ Distance: _____ Elev:_____

_____ Distance: _____ Elev:_____

Places We Saw:

_____

_____

_____

Places We Stayed:

_____

_____

_____

Dates We Visited:

_____ - _____

_____ - _____

Our Favorite Memory:

_____
_____
_____
_____
_____
_____

Things we learned:

_____
_____
_____
_____
_____
_____
_____
_____
_____
_____
_____
_____

Notes For Next Time:

_____
_____
_____
_____
_____
_____
_____
_____
_____
_____

LASSEN VOLCANIC NATIONAL PARK

(Park Sign or Photo Here)

Trails We Hiked:

_____ Distance: _____ Elev:_____

_____ Distance: _____ Elev:_____

_____ Distance: _____ Elev:_____

_____ Distance: _____ Elev:_____

Places We Saw:

_____

_____

_____

Places We Stayed:

_____

_____

_____

Dates We Visited:

_____ - _____
_____ - _____

Our Favorite Memory:

_____
_____
_____
_____
_____
_____

Things we learned:

_____
_____
_____
_____
_____
_____
_____
_____
_____
_____
_____
_____

Notes For Next Time:

_____
_____
_____
_____
_____
_____
_____
_____
_____
_____

MAMMOTH CAVE NATIONAL PARK

(Park Sign or Photo Here)

Trails We Hiked:

_____ Distance: _____ Elev:_____

_____ Distance: _____ Elev:_____

_____ Distance: _____ Elev:_____

_____ Distance: _____ Elev:_____

Places We Saw:

_____

_____

_____

Places We Stayed:

_____

_____

_____

Dates We Visited:

_____ - _____

_____ - _____

Our Favorite Memory:

_____
_____
_____
_____
_____
_____

Things we learned:

_____
_____
_____
_____
_____
_____
_____
_____
_____
_____
_____
_____

Notes For Next Time:

_____
_____
_____
_____
_____
_____
_____
_____
_____

MESA VERDE NATIONAL PARK

(Park Sign or Photo Here)

Trails We Hiked:

_____ Distance: _____ Elev:_____

_____ Distance: _____ Elev:_____

_____ Distance: _____ Elev:_____

_____ Distance: _____ Elev:_____

Places We Saw:

_____

_____

_____

Places We Stayed:

_____

_____

_____

Dates We Visited:

_____ - _____
_____ - _____

Our Favorite Memory:

_____
_____
_____
_____
_____

Things we learned:

_____
_____
_____
_____
_____
_____
_____
_____
_____
_____
_____

Notes For Next Time:

_____
_____
_____
_____
_____
_____
_____
_____
_____

MOUNT RAINIER NATIONAL PARK

(Park Sign or Photo Here)

Trails We Hiked:

_____ Distance: _____ Elev:_____

_____ Distance: _____ Elev:_____

_____ Distance: _____ Elev:_____

_____ Distance: _____ Elev:_____

Places We Saw:

_____

_____

_____

Places We Stayed:

_____

_____

_____

Dates We Visited:

_____ - _____

_____ - _____

Our Favorite Memory:

_____

_____

_____

_____

_____

Things we learned:

_____

_____

_____

_____

_____

_____

_____

_____

_____

Notes For Next Time:

_____

_____

_____

_____

_____

_____

_____

_____

NATIONAL PARK OF AMERICAN SAMOA

(Park Sign or Photo Here)

Trails We Hiked:

_____ Distance: _____ Elev:_____

_____ Distance: _____ Elev:_____

_____ Distance: _____ Elev:_____

_____ Distance: _____ Elev:_____

Places We Saw:

_____

_____

_____

Places We Stayed:

_____

_____

_____

Dates We Visited:

_____ - _____
_____ - _____

Our Favorite Memory:

_____
_____
_____
_____
_____

Things we learned:

_____
_____
_____
_____
_____
_____
_____
_____
_____
_____
_____

Notes For Next Time:

_____
_____
_____
_____
_____
_____
_____
_____
_____

NEW RIVER GORGE NATIONAL PARK

(Park Sign or Photo Here)

Trails We Hiked:

_____ Distance: _____ Elev:_____

_____ Distance: _____ Elev:_____

_____ Distance: _____ Elev:_____

_____ Distance: _____ Elev:_____

Places We Saw:

_____

_____

_____

Places We Stayed:

_____

_____

_____

Dates We Visited:

_____ - _____

_____ - _____

Our Favorite Memory:

_____

_____

_____

_____

_____

Things we learned:

_____

_____

_____

_____

_____

_____

_____

_____

_____

_____

Notes For Next Time:

_____

_____

_____

_____

_____

_____

_____

_____

NORTH CASCADES NATIONAL PARK

(Park Sign or Photo Here)

Trails We Hiked:

_____ Distance: _____ Elev:_____

_____ Distance: _____ Elev:_____

_____ Distance: _____ Elev:_____

_____ Distance: _____ Elev:_____

Places We Saw:

_____

_____

_____

Places We Stayed:

_____

_____

_____

_____ - _____

_____ - _____

Our Favorite Memory:

_____
_____
_____
_____
_____

Things we learned:

_____
_____
_____
_____
_____
_____
_____
_____
_____
_____

Notes For Next Time:

_____
_____
_____
_____
_____
_____
_____
_____
_____

OLYMPIC NATIONAL PARK

(Park Sign or Photo Here)

Trails We Hiked:

_____ Distance: _____ Elev:_____

_____ Distance: _____ Elev:_____

_____ Distance: _____ Elev:_____

_____ Distance: _____ Elev:_____

Places We Saw:

_____

_____

_____

Places We Stayed:

_____

_____

_____

Dates We Visited:

_____ - _____
_____ - _____

Our Favorite Memory:

_____
_____
_____
_____
_____
_____

Things we learned:

_____
_____
_____
_____
_____
_____
_____
_____
_____
_____
_____

Notes For Next Time:

_____
_____
_____
_____
_____
_____
_____
_____
_____

PETRIFIED FOREST NATIONAL PARK

(Park Sign or Photo Here)

Trails We Hiked:

_____ Distance: _____ Elev:_____

_____ Distance: _____ Elev:_____

_____ Distance: _____ Elev:_____

_____ Distance: _____ Elev:_____

Places We Saw:

_____

_____

_____

Places We Stayed:

_____

_____

_____

Dates We Visited:

_____ - _____

_____ - _____

Our Favorite Memory:

_____
_____
_____
_____
_____
_____

Things we learned:

_____
_____
_____
_____
_____
_____
_____
_____
_____
_____
_____
_____

Notes For Next Time:

_____
_____
_____
_____
_____
_____
_____
_____
_____

PINNACLES NATIONAL PARK

(Park Sign or Photo Here)

Trails We Hiked:

_____ Distance: _____ Elev:_____

_____ Distance: _____ Elev:_____

_____ Distance: _____ Elev:_____

_____ Distance: _____ Elev:_____

Places We Saw:

_____

_____

_____

Places We Stayed:

_____

_____

_____

Dates We Visited:

_____ - _____

_____ - _____

Our Favorite Memory:

_____

_____

_____

_____

_____

Things we learned:

_____

_____

_____

_____

_____

_____

_____

_____

_____

_____

Notes For Next Time:

_____

_____

_____

_____

_____

_____

_____

_____

_____

REDWOOD NATIONAL PARK

(Park Sign or Photo Here)

Trails We Hiked:

_____ Distance: _____ Elev:_____

_____ Distance: _____ Elev:_____

_____ Distance: _____ Elev:_____

_____ Distance: _____ Elev:_____

Places We Saw:

_____

_____

_____

Places We Stayed:

_____

_____

_____

Dates We Visited:

_____ - _____

_____ - _____

Our Favorite Memory:

_____
_____
_____
_____
_____
_____

Things we learned:

_____
_____
_____
_____
_____
_____
_____
_____
_____
_____
_____

Notes For Next Time:

_____
_____
_____
_____
_____
_____
_____
_____
_____

ROCKY MOUNTAIN NATIONAL PARK

(Park Sign or Photo Here)

Trails We Hiked:

_____ Distance: _____ Elev:_____

_____ Distance: _____ Elev:_____

_____ Distance: _____ Elev:_____

_____ Distance: _____ Elev:_____

Places We Saw:

_____

_____

_____

Places We Stayed:

_____

_____

_____

Dates We Visited:

_____ - _____
_____ - _____

Our Favorite Memory:

_____
_____
_____
_____
_____

Things we learned:

_____
_____
_____
_____
_____
_____
_____
_____
_____
_____

Notes For Next Time:

_____
_____
_____
_____
_____
_____
_____
_____

SAGUARO NATIONAL PARK

(Park Sign or Photo Here)

Trails We Hiked:

_____ Distance: _____ Elev:_____

_____ Distance: _____ Elev:_____

_____ Distance: _____ Elev:_____

_____ Distance: _____ Elev:_____

Places We Saw:

_____

_____

_____

Places We Stayed:

_____

_____

_____

Dates We Visited:

_____ - _____

_____ - _____

Our Favorite Memory:

_____
_____
_____
_____
_____

Things we learned:

_____
_____
_____
_____
_____
_____
_____
_____
_____
_____

Notes For Next Time:

_____
_____
_____
_____
_____
_____
_____
_____
_____

SEQUOIA NATIONAL PARK

(Park Sign or Photo Here)

Trails We Hiked:

_____ Distance: _____ Elev:_____

_____ Distance: _____ Elev:_____

_____ Distance: _____ Elev:_____

_____ Distance: _____ Elev:_____

Places We Saw:

_____

_____

_____

Places We Stayed:

_____

_____

_____

Dates We Visited:

_____ - _____

_____ - _____

Our Favorite Memory:

_____
_____
_____
_____
_____
_____

Things we learned:

_____
_____
_____
_____
_____
_____
_____
_____
_____
_____
_____

Notes For Next Time:

_____
_____
_____
_____
_____
_____
_____
_____
_____

SHENANDOAH NATIONAL PARK

(Park Sign or Photo Here)

Trails We Hiked:

_____ Distance: _____ Elev:_____

_____ Distance: _____ Elev:_____

_____ Distance: _____ Elev:_____

_____ Distance: _____ Elev:_____

Places We Saw:

_____

_____

_____

Places We Stayed:

_____

_____

Dates We Visited:

_____ - _____
_____ - _____

Our Favorite Memory:

_____
_____
_____
_____
_____

Things we learned:

_____
_____
_____
_____
_____
_____
_____
_____
_____
_____

Notes For Next Time:

_____
_____
_____
_____
_____
_____
_____
_____

THEODORE ROOSEVELT NATIONAL PARK

(Park Sign or Photo Here)

Trails We Hiked:

_____ Distance: _____ Elev:_____

_____ Distance: _____ Elev:_____

_____ Distance: _____ Elev:_____

_____ Distance: _____ Elev:_____

Places We Saw:

_____

_____

_____

Places We Stayed:

_____

_____

_____

_____ - _____

_____ - _____

Our Favorite Memory:

_____
_____
_____
_____
_____
_____

Things we learned:

_____
_____
_____
_____
_____
_____
_____
_____
_____
_____
_____

Notes For Next Time:

_____
_____
_____
_____
_____
_____
_____
_____
_____

VIRGIN ISLANDS NATIONAL PARK

(Park Sign or Photo Here)

Trails We Hiked:

_____ Distance: _____ Elev:_____

_____ Distance: _____ Elev:_____

_____ Distance: _____ Elev:_____

_____ Distance: _____ Elev:_____

Places We Saw:

_____

_____

_____

Places We Stayed:

_____

_____

_____

Dates We Visited:

_____ - _____
_____ - _____

Our Favorite Memory:

_____
_____
_____
_____
_____
_____

Things we learned:

_____
_____
_____
_____
_____
_____
_____
_____
_____
_____
_____
_____

Notes For Next Time:

_____
_____
_____
_____
_____
_____
_____
_____
_____

VOYAGEURS NATIONAL PARK

(Park Sign or Photo Here)

Trails We Hiked:

_____ Distance: _____ Elev:_____

_____ Distance: _____ Elev:_____

_____ Distance: _____ Elev:_____

_____ Distance: _____ Elev:_____

Places We Saw:

_____

_____

_____

Places We Stayed:

_____

_____

_____

Dates We Visited:

_____ - _____

_____ - _____

Our Favorite Memory:

_____
_____
_____
_____
_____

Things we learned:

_____
_____
_____
_____
_____
_____
_____
_____
_____
_____

Notes For Next Time:

_____
_____
_____
_____
_____
_____
_____
_____
_____

WHITE SANDS NATIONAL PARK

(Park Sign or Photo Here)

Trails We Hiked:

_____ Distance: _____ Elev:_____

_____ Distance: _____ Elev:_____

_____ Distance: _____ Elev:_____

_____ Distance: _____ Elev:_____

Places We Saw:

_____

_____

_____

Places We Stayed:

_____

_____

_____

Dates We Visited:

_____ - _____

_____ - _____

Our Favorite Memory:

_____
_____
_____
_____
_____

Things we learned:

_____
_____
_____
_____
_____
_____
_____
_____
_____
_____
_____

Notes For Next Time:

_____
_____
_____
_____
_____
_____
_____
_____
_____

WIND CAVE NATIONAL PARK

(Park Sign or Photo Here)

Trails We Hiked:

_____ Distance: _____ Elev:_____

_____ Distance: _____ Elev:_____

_____ Distance: _____ Elev:_____

_____ Distance: _____ Elev:_____

Places We Saw:

_____

_____

_____

Places We Stayed:

_____

_____

_____

Dates We Visited:

_____ - _____
_____ - _____

Our Favorite Memory:

_____
_____
_____
_____
_____

Things we learned:

_____
_____
_____
_____
_____
_____
_____
_____
_____
_____
_____

Notes For Next Time:

_____
_____
_____
_____
_____
_____
_____
_____
_____

WRANGELL-ST. ELIAS NATIONAL PARK

(Park Sign or Photo Here)

Trails We Hiked:

_____ Distance: _____ Elev:_____

_____ Distance: _____ Elev:_____

_____ Distance: _____ Elev:_____

_____ Distance: _____ Elev:_____

Places We Saw:

_____

_____

_____

Places We Stayed:

_____

_____

_____

Dates We Visited:

_____ - _____
_____ - _____

Our Favorite Memory:

_____
_____
_____
_____
_____

Things we learned:

_____
_____
_____
_____
_____
_____
_____
_____
_____
_____
_____

Notes For Next Time:

_____
_____
_____
_____
_____
_____
_____
_____
_____

YELLOWSTONE NATIONAL PARK

(Park Sign or Photo Here)

Trails We Hiked:

_____ Distance: _____ Elev:_____

_____ Distance: _____ Elev:_____

_____ Distance: _____ Elev:_____

_____ Distance: _____ Elev:_____

Places We Saw:

_____

_____

_____

Places We Stayed:

_____

_____

_____

Dates We Visited:

_____ - _____

_____ - _____

Our Favorite Memory:

_____

_____

_____

_____

_____

Things we learned:

_____

_____

_____

_____

_____

_____

_____

_____

_____

_____

Notes For Next Time:

_____

_____

_____

_____

_____

_____

_____

_____

YOSEMITE NATIONAL PARK

(Park Sign or Photo Here)

Trails We Hiked:

_____ Distance: _____ Elev:_____

_____ Distance: _____ Elev:_____

_____ Distance: _____ Elev:_____

_____ Distance: _____ Elev:_____

Places We Saw: **Places We Stayed:**

_____   _____

_____   _____

_____   _____

Dates We Visited:

_____ - _____

_____ - _____

Our Favorite Memory:

_____
_____
_____
_____
_____

Things we learned:

_____
_____
_____
_____
_____
_____
_____
_____
_____
_____
_____

Notes For Next Time:

_____
_____
_____
_____
_____
_____
_____
_____
_____

ZION NATIONAL PARK

(Park Sign or Photo Here)

Trails We Hiked:

_____ Distance: _____ Elev:_____

_____ Distance: _____ Elev:_____

_____ Distance: _____ Elev:_____

_____ Distance: _____ Elev:_____

Places We Saw:

_____

_____

_____

Places We Stayed:

_____

_____

_____

Dates We Visited:

_____ - _____
_____ - _____

Our Favorite Memory:

_____
_____
_____
_____
_____

Things we learned:

_____
_____
_____
_____
_____
_____
_____
_____
_____
_____
_____

Notes For Next Time:

_____
_____
_____
_____
_____
_____
_____
_____
_____

ADDITIONAL
NATIONAL PARK SERVICE
SITES

NATIONAL MONUMENTS

ALABAMA:	DATE OF VISIT	FLORIDA:	DATE OF VISIT
Birmingham Civil Rights	_____	Castillo de San Marcos	_____
Freedom Riders	_____	Fort Matanzas	_____
Russel Cave	_____		
		GEORGIA:	
ALASKA:		Fort Frederica	_____
Aniakchak	_____	Fort Pulaski	_____
Cape Krusenstern	_____		
		IDAHO:	
ARIZONA:		Craters Of The Moon	_____
Canyon de Chelly	_____	Hagerman Fossil Beds	_____
Casa Grande Ruins	_____		
Chiricahua	_____	ILLINOIS:	
Coronado	_____	Pullman	_____
Grand Canyon Parashant	_____		
Montezuma Castle	_____	IOWA:	
Navajo	_____	Effigy Mounds	_____
Organ Pipe Cactus	_____		
Pipe Spring	_____	KENTUCKY:	
Sunset Crater Volcano	_____	Camp Nelson	_____
Tonto	_____	Mill Springs Battlefield	_____
Tuzigoot	_____		
Walnut Canyon	_____	LOUISIANA:	
Wutpatki	_____	Poverty Port	_____
CALIFORNIA:		MAINE:	
Cabrillo	_____	Katahdin Woods and Waters	_____
Castle Mountains	_____		
Cesar E. Chavez	_____	MARYLAND:	
Devil's Postpile	_____	Fort McHenry	_____
Lava Beds	_____		
Muir Woods	_____	MINNESOTA:	
Tule Lake	_____	Grand Portage	_____
		Pipestone	_____
COLORADO:			
Colorado	_____	MISSISSIPPI:	
Dinosaur	_____	Medgar and Myrlie Evers Home	_____
Florissant Fossil Beds	_____		
Yucca House	_____	MISSOURI:	
		George Washington Carver	_____

NATIONAL MONUMENTS

MONTANA:	DATE OF VISIT	TEXAS:	DATE OF VISIT
Little Bighorn Battlefield	_____	Alibates Flint Quarries	_____
		Waco Mammoth	_____
NEBRASKA:			
Agate Fossil Beds	_____	**UTAH:**	
Scotts Bluffs	_____	Cedar Breaks	_____
		Hovenweep	_____
NEVADA:		Natural Bridges	_____
Tule Springs Fossil Beds	_____	Rainbow Bridge	_____
		Timpanogos Cave	_____
NEW MEXICO:			
Aztec Ruins	_____	**VIRGIN ISLANDS:**	
Bandelier	_____	Buck Island Reef	_____
Capulin Volcano	_____	Virgin Islands Coral Reef	_____
El Malpais	_____		
El Morro	_____	**VIRGINIA:**	
Fort Union	_____	Booker T Washington	_____
Gila Cliff Dwellings	_____	Fort Monroe	_____
Petroglyph	_____	George Washington Birthplace	_____
Salinas Pueblo Missions	_____		
		WYOMING:	
NEW YORK:		Devils Tower	_____
African Burial Ground	_____	Fossil Butte	_____
Castle Clinton	_____		
Ellis Island	_____		
Fort Stanwix	_____		
Governors Island	_____		
Statue of Liberty	_____		
Stonewall	_____		
OHIO:			
Charles Young Buffalo Soldiers	_____		
OREGON:			
John Day Fossil Beds	_____		
Oregon Caves	_____		
SOUTH DAKOTA:			
Jewel Cave	_____		

NATIONAL SEASHORES

NATIONAL LAKESHORES

NATIONAL RECREATION AREAS

Amistad National Recreation Area

Bighorn Canyon National Recreation Area

Boston Harbor Islands National Recreation Area

Chattahoochee River National Recreation Area

Chickasaw National Recreation Area

Curecanti National Recreation Area

Delaware Water Gap National Recreation Area

Gateway National Recreation Area

Gauley River National Recreation Area

Glen Canyon National Recreation Area

Golden Gate National Recreation Area

Lake Chelan National Recreation Area

Lake Mead National Recreation Area

Lake Meredith National Recreation Area

Lake Roosevelt National Recreation Area

Ross Lake National Recreation Area

Santa Monica Mountains National Recreation Area

Whiskeytown-Shasta-Trinity National Recreation Area

NATIONAL HISTORICAL PARKS

ALASKA:	DATE OF VISIT	LOUISIANA:	DATE OF VISIT
Klondike Gold Rush		Cane River Creole	
Sitka		Jean Lafitte	
		New Orleans Jazz	
ARIZONA:			
Tumacacori		MARYLAND:	
		Chesapeake and Ohio Canal	
CALIFORNIA:		Harriet Tubman Underground Railroad	
Rosie the Riveter WWII Home Front			
San Francisco Maritime		MASSACHUSETTS:	
		Adams	
CONNECTICUT:		Boston	
Weir Farm		Lowell	
		Minute Man	
DELAWARE:		New Bedford Whaling	
First State			
		MICHIGAN:	
GEORGIA:		Keweenaw	
Jimmy Carter			
Martin Luther King, Jr.		MISSISSIPPI:	
Ocmulgee Mounds		Natchez	
GUAM:		MISSOURI:	
War in the Pacific		Ste. Genevieve	
HAWAII:		NEBRASKA:	
Kalaupapa		Homestead	
Kaloko-Honokohau			
Pu'uhonua o Honaunau		NEW HAMPSHIRE:	
		Saint Gaudens	
IDAHO:			
Nez Perce		NEW JERSEY:	
		Morristown	
INDIANA:		Paterson Great Falls	
George Rogers Clark		Thomas Edison	
KENTUCKY:		NEW MEXICO:	
Abraham Lincoln Birthplace		Chaco Culture	
Cumberland Gap		Manhattan Project	
		Pecos	

NATIONAL HISTORICAL PARKS

NEW YORK: DATE OF VISIT

Harriet Tubman   _____
Saratoga   _____
Women's Rights   _____

OHIO:

Dayton Aviation Heritage   _____
Hopewell Culture   _____

OREGON:

Lewis and Clark   _____

PENNSYLVANIA:

Independence   _____
Valley Forge   _____

RHODE ISLAND:

Blackstone River Valley   _____

SOUTH CAROLINA:

Fort Sumter and Fort Moultrie   _____
Reconstruction Era   _____

TEXAS:

Lyndon B. Johnson   _____
Palo Alto Battlefield   _____
San Antonio Missions   _____

UTAH:

Golden Spike   _____

VERMONT:

Marsh-Billings-Rockefeller   _____

VIRGIN ISLANDS:

Salt River Bay   _____

VIRGINIA: DATE OF VISIT

Appomattox Court House   _____
Cedar Creek and Belle Grove   _____
Colonial   _____

WASHINGTON:

San Juan Island   _____

WEST VIRGINIA:

Harpers Ferry   _____

NATIONAL HISTORIC SITES

ALABAMA:	DATE OF VISIT	IDAHO:	DATE OF VISIT
Tuskegee Airmen	_____	Minidoka	_____
Tuskegee Institute	_____		
		ILLINOIS:	
ARIZONA:		Lincoln Home	_____
Fort Bowie	_____		
Hubbell Trading Post	_____	IOWA:	
		Herbert Hoover	_____
ARKANSAS:			
Fort Smith	_____	KANSAS:	
Little Rock Central High School	_____	Brown v. Board of Education	_____
President Clinton Birthplace Home	_____	Fort Larned	_____
		Fort Scott	_____
CALIFORNIA:		Nicodemus	_____
Eugene O'Neill	_____		
Fort Point	_____	MARYLAND:	
John Muir	_____	Clara Barton	_____
Manzanar	_____	Hampton	_____
		Thomas Stone	_____
COLORADO:			
Bent's Old Fort	_____	MASSACHUSETTS:	
Sand Creek Massacre	_____	Boston African American	_____
		Frederick Law Olmsted	_____
DISTRICT OF COLUMBIA:		John Fitzgerald Kennedy	_____
Carter G. Woodson Home	_____	Longfellow Washington's Headquarters	_____
Ford's Theatre	_____	Salem Maritime	_____
Frederick Douglass	_____	Saugus Iron Works	_____
Mary McLeod Bethune Council House	_____	Springfield Armory	_____
Pennsylvania Avenue	_____		
		MISSOURI:	
GEORGIA:		Harry S Truman	_____
Andersonville	_____	Ulysses S. Grant	_____
HAWAII:		MONTANA:	
Honouliuli	_____	Grant-Kohrs Ranch	_____
Pu'ukohola Heiau	_____		

NATIONAL HISTORIC SITES

NEW YORK:
DATE OF VISIT

Eleanor Roosevelt _____
Home of Franklin D. Roosevelt _____
Martin Van Buren _____
Sagamore Hill _____
Saint Paul's Church _____
Theodore Roosevelt Birthplace _____
Theodore Roosevelt Inaugural _____
Vanderbilt Mansion _____

NORTH CAROLINA:

Carl Sandburg Home _____
Fort Raleigh _____

NORTH DAKOTA:

Fort Union-Trading Post _____
Knife River Indian Villages _____

OHIO:

First Ladies _____
James A. Garfield _____
William Howard Taft _____

OKLAHOMA:

Washita Battlefield _____

PENNSYLVANIA:

Allegheny Portage Railroad _____
Edgar Allan Poe _____
Eisenhower _____
Friendship Hill _____
Hopewell Furnace _____
Steamtown _____

PUERTO RICO:

San Juan _____

SOUTH CAROLINA:

Charles Pinckney _____
Ninety Six _____

SOUTH DAKOTA:
DATE OF VISIT

Minuteman Missile _____

TENNESSEE:

Andrew Johnson _____

TEXAS:

Fort Davis _____

VIRGIN ISLANDS:

Christiansted _____

VIRGINIA:

Maggie L. Walker _____

WASHINGTON:

Fort Vancouver _____
Whitman Mission _____

WYOMING:

Fort Laramie _____

NATIONAL MEMORIALS

DATE OF VISIT

Arkansas Post National Memorial _____

Arlington House, The Robert E. Lee Memorial _____

Chamizal National Memorial _____

Coronado National Memorial _____

Dwight D. Eisenhower Memorial _____

De Soto National Memorial _____

Federal Hall National Memorial _____

Flight 93 National Memorial _____

Fort Caroline National Memorial _____

Franklin Delano Roosevelt Memorial _____

General Grant National Memorial _____

Hamilton Grange National Memorial _____

Johnstown Flood National Memorial _____

Korean War Veterans Memorial _____

Lincoln Boyhood National Memorial _____

Lincoln Memorial _____

Lyndon Baines Johnson Memorial Grove on the Potomac _____

Martin Luther King Jr. Memorial _____

Mount Rushmore National Memorial _____

Pearl Harbor National Memorial _____

Perry's Victory and International Peace Memorial _____

Port Chicago Naval Magazine National Memorial _____

Roger Williams National Memorial _____

Thaddeus Kosciuszko National Memorial _____

Theodore Roosevelt Island _____

Thomas Jefferson Memorial _____

Vietnam Veterans Memorial _____

Washington Monument _____

World War I Memorial _____

World War II Memorial _____

Wright Brothers National Memorial _____

NATIONAL BATTLEFIELDS

NATIONAL BATTLEFIELD PARKS AND SITES

Made in the USA
Monee, IL
15 June 2023

e433cba7-5f50-41ba-bd00-129b09666713R01